EASY PIANO

MY FIRST HYMNS SONG BOOK

A TREASURY OF FAVORITE SONGS TO PLAY

ISBN 978-1-4803-9389-9

HAL•LEONARD®
CORPORATION
7777 W. BLUEMOUND RD. P.O. BOX 13819 MILWAUKEE, WI 53213

In Australia Contact:
Hal Leonard Australia Pty. Ltd.
4 Lentara Court
Cheltenham, Victoria, 3192 Australia
Email: ausadmin@halleonard.com.au

For all works contained herein:
Unauthorized copying, arranging, adapting, recording, Internet posting, public performance,
or other distribution of the printed music in this publication is an infringement of copyright.
Infringers are liable under the law.

Visit Hal Leonard Online at
www.halleonard.com

Amazing Grace

Words by JOHN NEWTON
Traditional American Melody

Slowly, with reverence

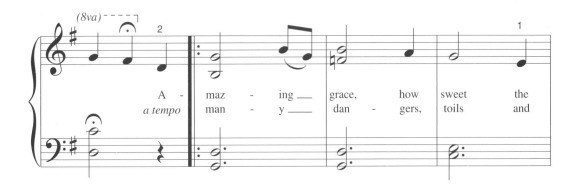

Copyright © 1995 by HAL LEONARD CORPORATION
International Copyright Secured   All Rights Reserved

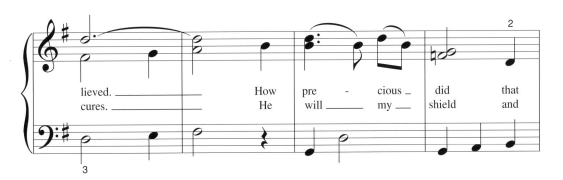

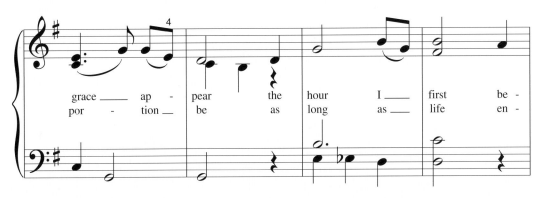

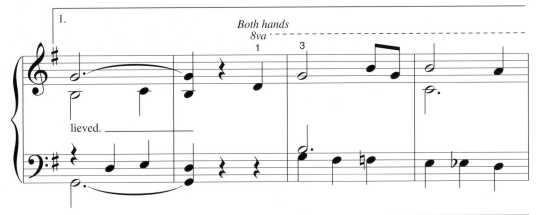

Be Thou My Vision

Traditional Irish
Translated by MARY E. BYRNE

Moderately

mf

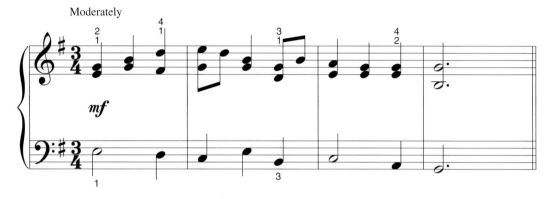

Be Thou my ____ vi - sion, O   Lord   of   my
Be Thou my ____ wis - dom, and   Thou   my   true
Great God of ____ heav - en, my   vic - to - ry

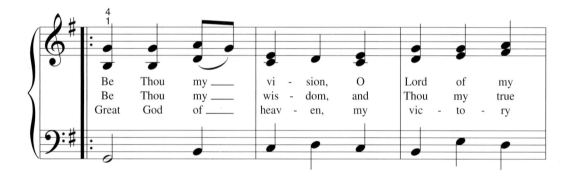

heart;   naught be all   else to me,   save that Thou
word;   I ev - er   with Thee and   Thou with me,
won,   may I reach   heav - en's joys,   O   bright heav'n's

Copyright © 2004 by HAL LEONARD CORPORATION
International Copyright Secured   All Rights Reserved

art.
Lord;
Sun!
Thou
Thou
Heart
my
and
of
best
Thou
my
thought,
on
own
by
ly,
heart, what-

day
first
ev
or
in
er
by
my
be-
night,
heart,
fall,
wak
great
still
ing
God
be
or
of
my

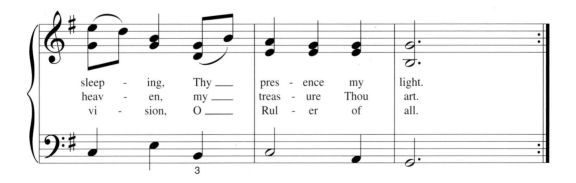

sleep
heav
vi
ing,
en,
sion,
Thy
my
O
pres
treas
Rul
ence
ure
er
my
Thou
of
light.
art.
all.

BLESSED ASSURANCE

Lyrics by FANNY J. CROSBY
Music by PHOEBE PALMER KNAPP

With movement

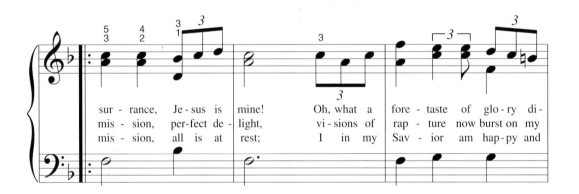

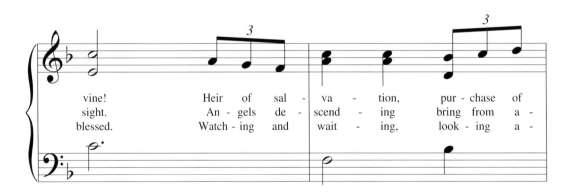

Copyright © 2002 by HAL LEONARD CORPORATION
International Copyright Secured   All Rights Reserved

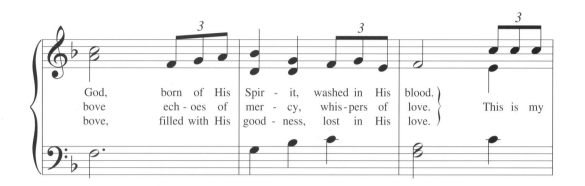

God, born of His Spir - it, washed in His blood.
bove ech - oes of mer - cy, whis - pers of love.
bove, filled with His good - ness, lost in His love.

This is my

sto - ry, this is my song, prais - ing my Sav - ior all the day

long. This is my sto - ry, this is my song, prais - ing my

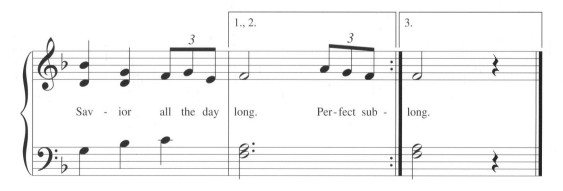

1., 2.

3.

Sav - ior all the day long. Per - fect sub - long.

Crown Him with Many Crowns

Words by MATTHEW BRIDGES and GODFREY THRING
Music by GEORGE JOB ELVEY

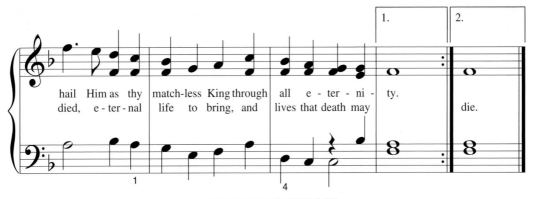

Copyright © 2014 by HAL LEONARD CORPORATION
International Copyright Secured   All Rights Reserved

Christ the Lord Is Risen Today

Words by CHARLES WESLEY
Music adapted from *Lyra Davidica*

Triumphantly

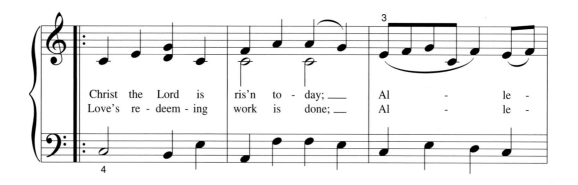

Christ the Lord is ris'n to-day; ___ Al - le - le -
Love's re-deem-ing work is done; ___ Al - le - le -

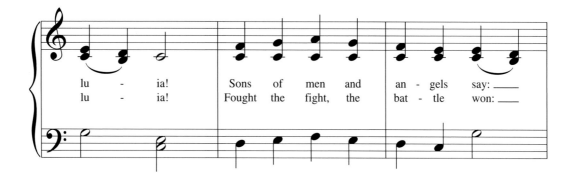

lu - ia! Sons of men and an - gels say: ___
lu - ia! Fought the fight, the bat - tle won: ___

Copyright © 2014 by HAL LEONARD CORPORATION
International Copyright Secured   All Rights Reserved

Al - le - lu - ia! Raise your joys and
Al - le - lu - ia! Vain the stone, the

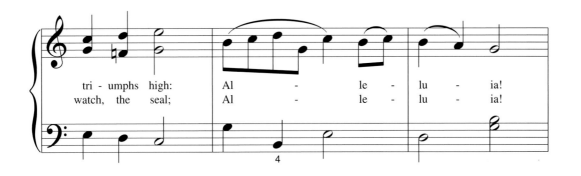

tri - umphs high: Al - le - lu - ia!
watch, the seal; Al - le - lu - ia!

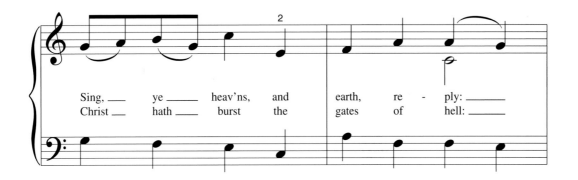

Sing, ___ ye ___ heav'ns, and earth, re - ply: ___
Christ ___ hath ___ burst the gates of hell: ___

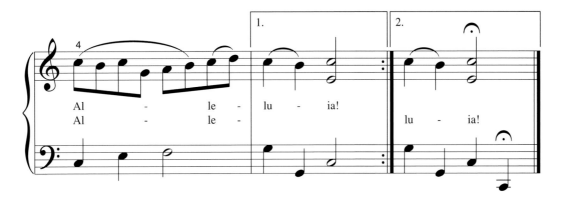

1.
Al - le - lu - ia!

2.
lu - ia!

For All the Saints

Words by WILLIAM W. HOW
Music by RALPH VAUGHAN WILLIAMS

Moderately

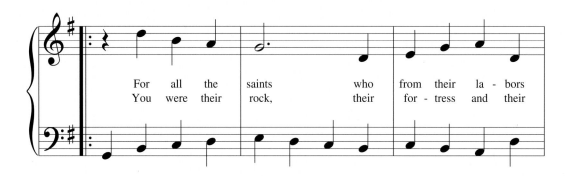

For all the saints, who from their la - bors
You were their rock, their for - tress and their

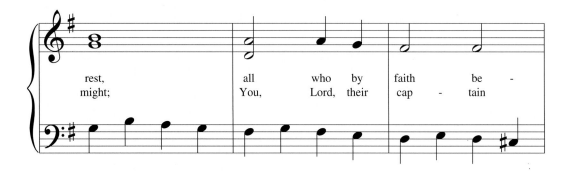

rest, all who by faith be -
might; You, Lord, their cap - tain

Copyright © 2014 by HAL LEONARD CORPORATION
International Copyright Secured   All Rights Reserved

fore the world con - fessed. Your name, O
in the well - fought fight. You, in the

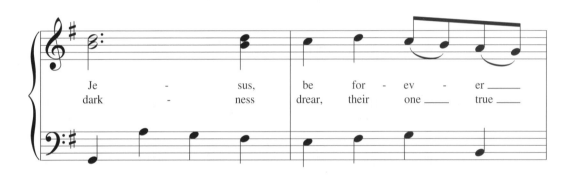

Je - sus, be for - ev - er _____
dark - ness drear, their one _____ true _____

blest. } Al - le - lu - ia! Al -
light. }

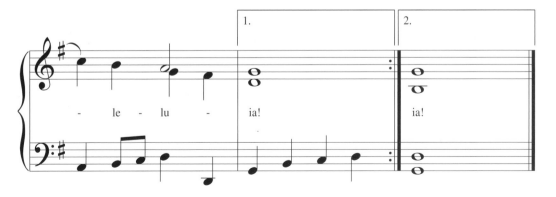

1.
- le - lu - ia!

2.
ia!

Fairest Lord Jesus

Words from *Münster Gesangbuch*
Verse 4 by JOSEPH A. SEISS
Music from *Schlesische Volkslieder*
Arranged by RICHARD STORRS WILLIS

Fair - est Lord
Fair - are the

Je - sus, rul - er of all na - ture,
mead - ows, fair - er still the wood - lands,

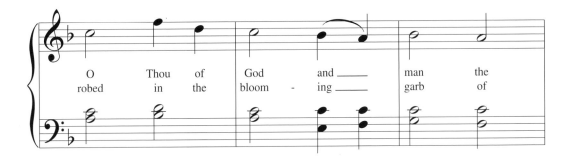

O Thou of God and ____ man the
robed in the bloom - ing ____ garb of

Copyright © 1992 by HAL LEONARD CORPORATION
International Copyright Secured   All Rights Reserved

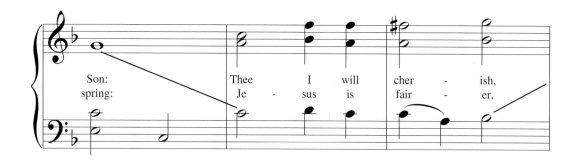

Son: Thee   I   will   cher - ish,
spring: Je - sus   is   fair - er,

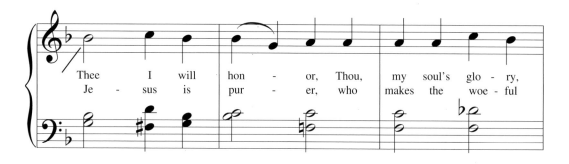

Thee   I   will   hon -   or, Thou, my soul's glo - ry,
Je - sus   is   pur -   er, who makes the woe - ful

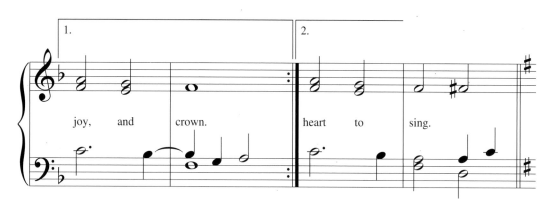

1.   joy, and   crown.   2.   heart to   sing.

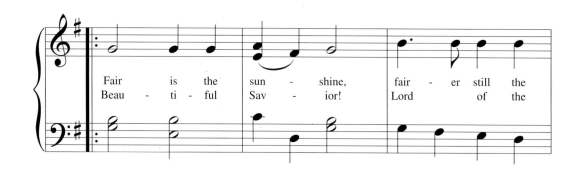

Fair   is   the   sun - shine,   fair - er still the
Beau - ti - ful Sav - ior!   Lord   of the

moon - light,   and   all   the   twin - kling _____
na - tions!   Son   of _____   God   and _____

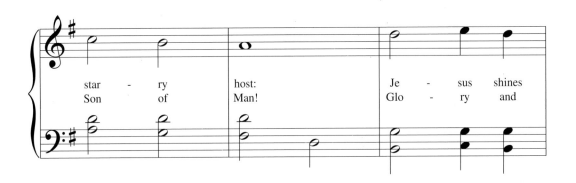

star - ry   host: Je - sus shines
Son   of   Man!   Glo - ry and

bright - er,   Je - sus shines pur - er than
hon - or,   praise,   ad - o - ra - tion, now

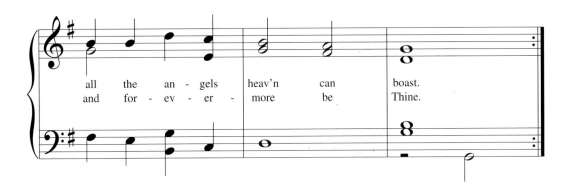

all   the   an - gels   heav'n   can   boast.
and   for - ev - er - more   be   Thine.

He Leadeth Me

Words by JOSEPH H. GILMORE
Music by WILLIAM B. BRADBURY

Moderately

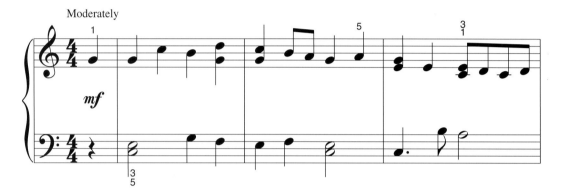

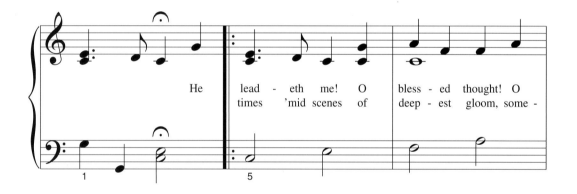

He lead - eth me! O bless - ed thought! O
times 'mid scenes of deep - est gloom, some -

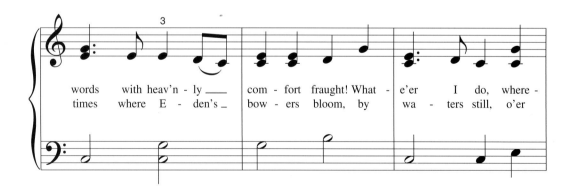

words with heav'n - ly ___ com - fort fraught! What - e'er I do, where -
times where E - den's ___ bow - ers bloom, by wa - ters still, o'er

Copyright © 2014 by HAL LEONARD CORPORATION
International Copyright Secured   All Rights Reserved

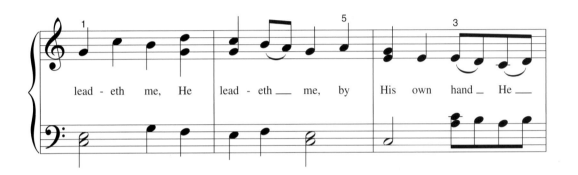

I Need Thee Every Hour

Words by ANNIE S. HAWKS
Music by ROBERT LOWRY

Gently, flowing

I need Thee ev - 'ry hour, most
need Thee ev - 'ry hour, most stay

gra - cious __ Lord; no ten - der voice like
Thou _____ near - by; temp - ta - tions lose their

Copyright © 2014 by HAL LEONARD CORPORATION
International Copyright Secured   All Rights Reserved

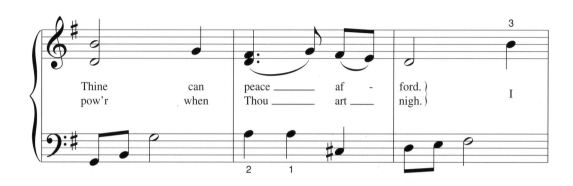

Thine   can   peace _____ af - ford.   3

pow'r   when   Thou _____ art ___ nigh.   I

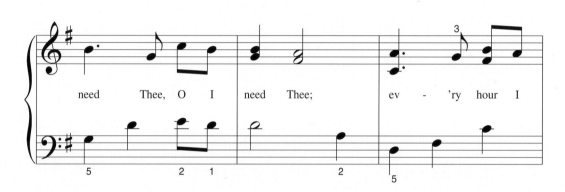

need   Thee,   O   I   need   Thee;   ev - 'ry   hour   I

need   Thee!   O   bless   me   now,   my   Sav - ior;   I

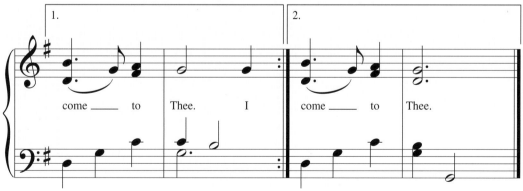

1.

come ___ to   Thee.   I

2.

come ___ to   Thee.

For the Beauty of the Earth

Words by FOLLIOT S. PIERPOINT
Music by CONRAD KOCHER

Moderately

For the beau-ty of the earth, for the glo-ry
For the won-der of each hour, of the day and

of the skies, for the love which from our birth
of the night, hill and vale and tree and flow'r,

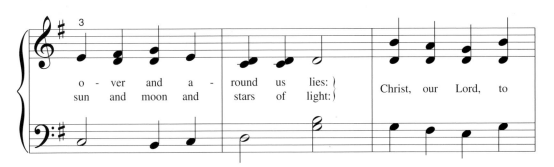

o-ver and a-round us lies: ⎱
sun and moon and stars of light: ⎰ Christ, our Lord, to

Thee we raise this, our hymn of grate-ful praise.

Copyright © 2014 by HAL LEONARD CORPORATION
International Copyright Secured   All Rights Reserved

In the Garden

Words and Music by
C. AUSTIN MILES

Moderately

come to the gar-den a - lone, _____ while the dew is
speaks, and the sound of His voice _____ is so sweet the

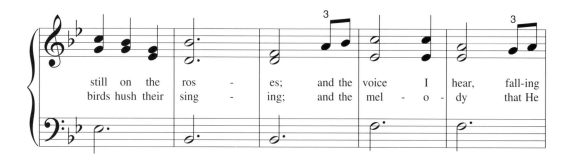

still on the ros - es; and the voice I hear, fall-ing
birds hush their sing - ing; and the mel - o - dy that He

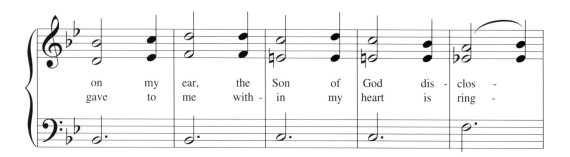

on my ear, the Son of God dis - clos -
gave to me with - in my heart is ring -

Copyright © 1999 by HAL LEONARD CORPORATION
International Copyright Secured   All Rights Reserved

es.
ing. } And He walks with me and He talks with

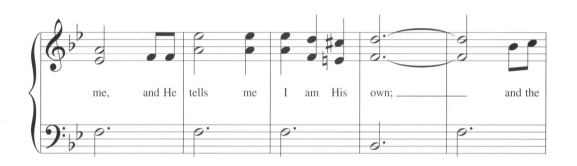

me, and He tells me I am His own; _____ and the

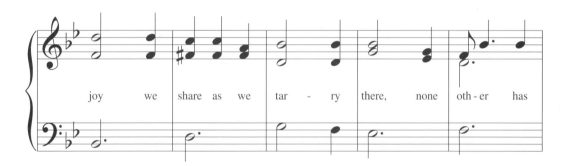

joy we share as we tar - ry there, none oth - er has

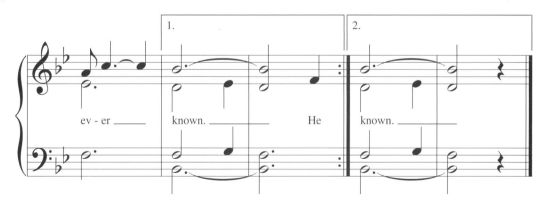

ev - er _____ known. _____ He   known. known.

IT IS WELL WITH MY SOUL

Words by HORATIO G. SPAFFORD
Music by PHILIP P. BLISS

Moderately

When peace like a riv - er at -
Sa - tan should buf - fet, though

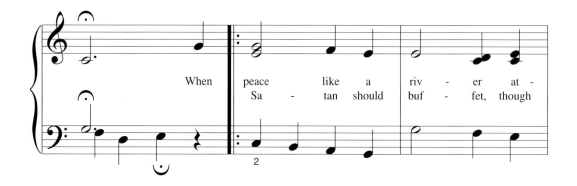

tend - eth my way, when sor - rows like sea bil - lows
tri - als should come, when let this blest as - sur - ance con -

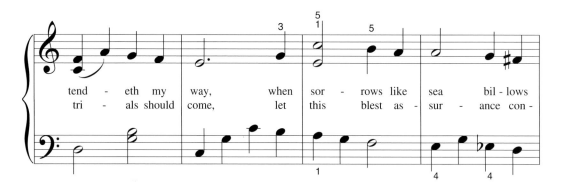

Copyright © 2014 by HAL LEONARD CORPORATION
International Copyright Secured   All Rights Reserved

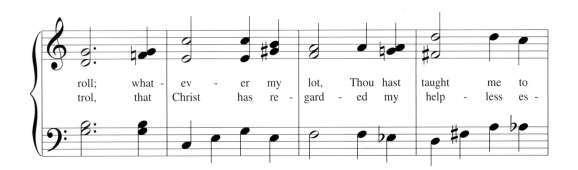

roll;   what – ev – er my   lot,   Thou hast   taught   me   to

trol,   that   Christ   has re – gard – ed   my   help – less   es –

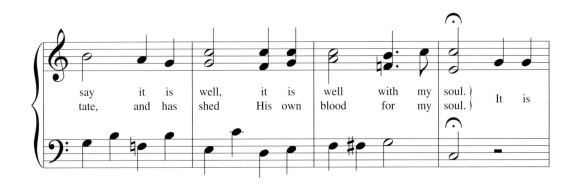

say   it is   well,   it is   well   with   my   soul.   It   is

tate,   and has   shed   His own   blood   for   my   soul.

well   (it is   well)   with   my   soul   (with   my   soul).   It is

well,   it is   well   with   my   soul.   Though   soul.

HOLY, HOLY, HOLY

Text by REGINALD HEBER
Music by JOHN B. DYKES

With dignity

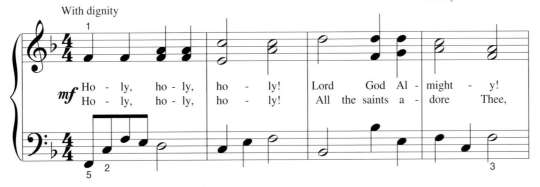

Holy, ho-ly, ho-ly! Lord God Al-might-y!
Ho-ly, ho-ly, ho-ly! All the saints a-dore Thee,

Ear-ly in the morn-ing our song shall rise to Thee.
cast-ing down their gold-en crowns a-round the glass-y sea.

Ho-ly, ho-ly, ho-ly! Mer-ci-ful and might-y,
Cher-u-bim and ser-a-phim fall-ing down be-fore Thee,

God in three per-sons, bless-ed Trin-i-ty!
which were, and are, and ev-er-more shall be.

Copyright © 1993 by HAL LEONARD PUBLISHING CORPORATION
International Copyright Secured   All Rights Reserved

Jesus Loves Me

Words by ANNA B. WARNER
Music by WILLIAM B. BRADBURY

Moderately, in 2

Je - sus loves me! This I know,
Je - sus loves me! This I know,
Je - sus loves me still to - day,

for the Bi - ble tells me so.
as He loved so long a - go,
walk - ing with me on my way,

Lit - tle ones to Him be - long;
tak - ing chil - dren on His knee,
want - ing as a friend to give

Copyright © 1993 by HAL LEONARD CORPORATION
International Copyright Secured   All Rights Reserved

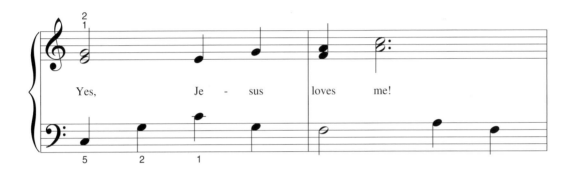

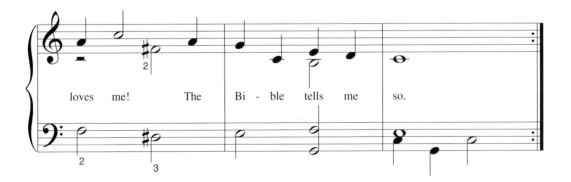

JUST AS I AM

Words by CHARLOTTE ELLIOTT
Music by WILLIAM B. BRADBURY

Moderately

Just —

as   I   am, ———— with - out ———— one
as   I   am, ———— and   wait - ing

plea,   but   that ———— Thy   blood   was
not   to   rid ———— my   soul   of

Copyright © 2014 by HAL LEONARD CORPORATION
International Copyright Secured   All Rights Reserved

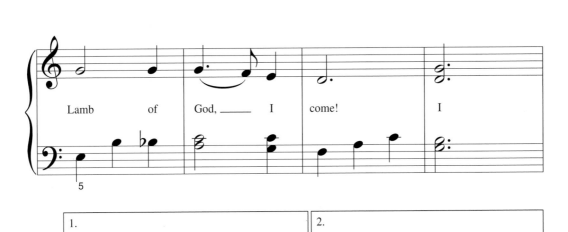

I Have Decided to Follow Jesus

Folk Melody from India
Arranged by AUILA READ

With spirit

mf

I have de-

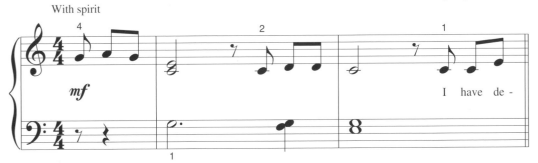

cid-ed ___ to fol-low Je - sus, I have de- cid-ed ___ to fol-low
hind me ___ the cross be- fore me, the world be- hind me, ___ the cross be-

Je - sus, I have de- cid-ed ___ to fol-low Je - sus,) no turn-ing
fore me, the world be- hind me, ___ the cross be- fore me,)

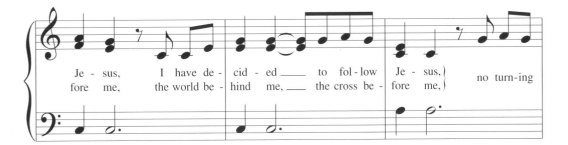

1.

2.

back, no turn-ing back. The world be - back.

Copyright © 2014 by HAL LEONARD CORPORATION
International Copyright Secured   All Rights Reserved

A Mighty Fortress Is Our God

Words and Music by MARTIN LUTHER
Translated by FREDERICK H. HEDGE
Based on Psalm 46

Majestically

A might-y for-tress
we in our ___ own

is ___ our God, a
strength ___ con - fide, our

bul - wark nev - er
striv - ing would be

fail - ing. Our
los - ing, were

help - er He, ___ a -
not the right ___ man

mid ___ the flood of
on ___ our side, the

mor - tal ills pre-
man of God's own

Copyright © 2014 by HAL LEONARD CORPORATION
International Copyright Secured All Rights Reserved

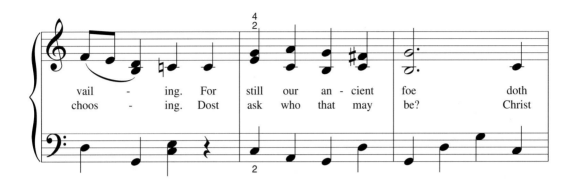

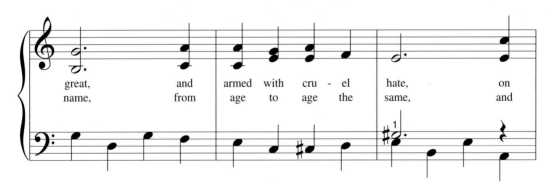

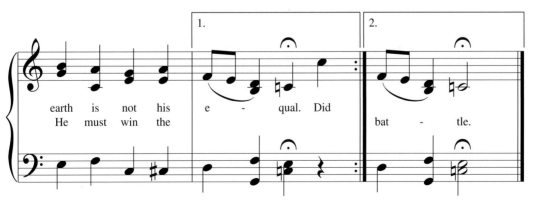

Praise to the Lord, the Almighty

Words by JOACHIM NEANDER
Translated by CATHERINE WINKWORTH
Music from *Erneuerten Gesangbuch*

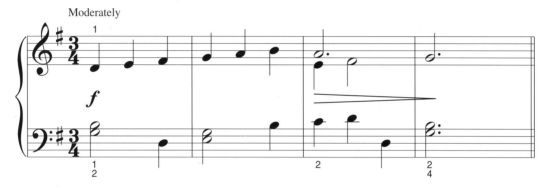

Praise to the Lord, the Al - might - y, the
Praise to the Lord, who o'er all things so

King of cre - a - tion! O my soul,
won - drous - ly reign - eth! Shel - ters thee

Copyright © 2014 by HAL LEONARD CORPORATION
International Copyright Secured   All Rights Reserved

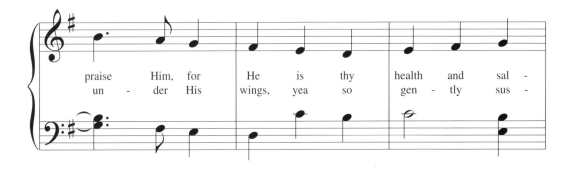

praise   Him,   for   He   is   thy   health   and   sal -
un -   der   His   wings, yea   so   gen - tly   sus -

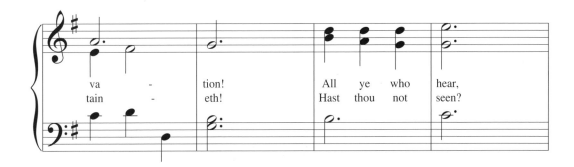

va -   tion!   All   ye   who   hear,
tain -   eth!   Hast thou not seen?

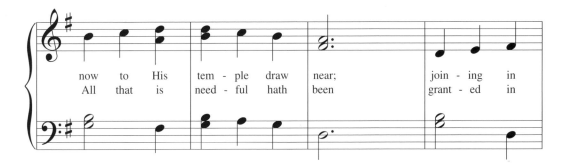

now   to   His   tem - ple draw near;   join - ing in
All   that   is   need - ful hath been   grant - ed in

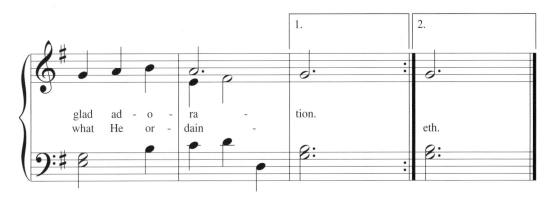

1.

2.

glad ad - o - ra -   tion.
what He or - dain -   eth.

Just a Closer Walk with Thee

Traditional
Arranged by KENNETH MORRIS

Slowly

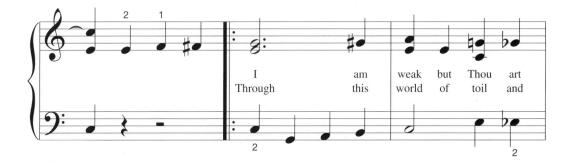

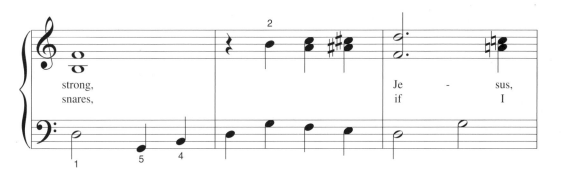

Copyright © 1993 by HAL LEONARD CORPORATION
International Copyright Secured   All Rights Reserved

I'll   be   sat - is - fied   as   long _____
Who   with   me   my   bur - den   shares? _____

_____   as   I   walk,   let   me   walk   close to
_____ None but   Thee,   dear   Lord,   none but

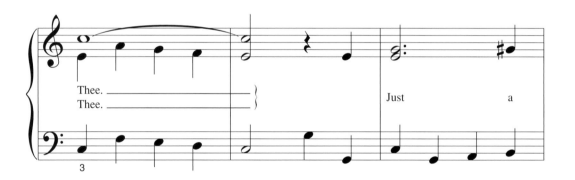

Thee. _____
Thee. _____   Just   a

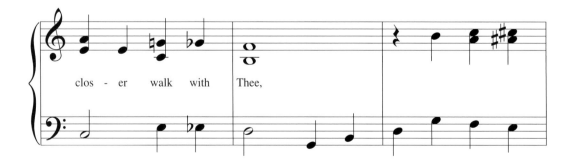

clos - er   walk   with   Thee,

grant it, Je - sus, is my plea. ___

Dai - ly walk - ing close to

Thee, ___ let it be, dear Lord, let it

1.
be. ___

2.
be. ___
rit.

Take My Life and Let It Be

Words by FRANCES R. HAVERGAL
Music by LOUIS J.F. HEROLD
Arranged by GEORGE KINGSLEY

Moderately

Take my life, and let it be
Take my voice, and let me sing
Take my will and make it Thine;

con - se - cra - ted, Lord, to Thee. Take my mo - ments
al - ways, on - ly, for my King. Take my lips, and
it shall be no long - er mine. Take my heart, it

Copyright © 2014 by HAL LEONARD CORPORATION
International Copyright Secured   All Rights Reserved

and my days; let them flow in cease - less praise.
let   them be filled with mes - sag - es from Thee.
is Thine own; it shall be Thy roy - al throne.

Take my hands, and let them move at the im - pulse
Take my sil - ver and my gold; not a mite would
Take my love, my Lord, I pour at Thy feet its

of Thy love. Take my feet, and let them be
I with- hold. Take my in - tel - lect, and use
treas - ure- store. Take my - self, and I will be

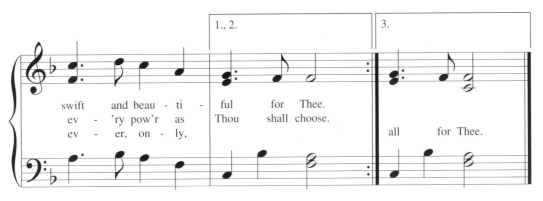

1., 2.   **3.**

swift and beau - ti - ful for Thee.
ev - 'ry pow'r as Thou shall choose.
ev - er, on - ly,   all for Thee.

We Gather Together

Words from *Nederlandtsch Gedenckclanck*
Translated by THEODORE BAKER
Netherlands Folk Melody
Arranged by EDWARD KREMSER

Moderately, sweetly

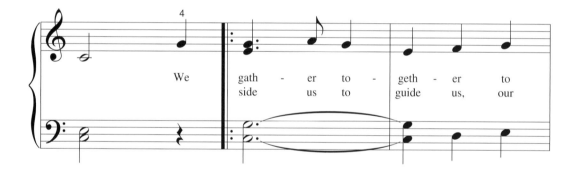

We gath – er to – geth – er to
side us to guide us, our

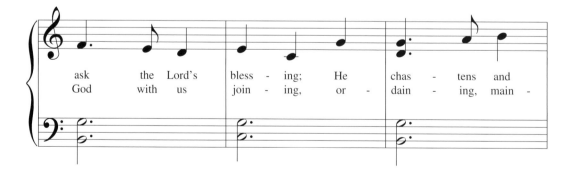

ask the Lord's bless – ing; He chas – tens and
God with us join – ing, or – dain – ing, main –

Copyright © 2014 by HAL LEONARD CORPORATION
International Copyright Secured   All Rights Reserved

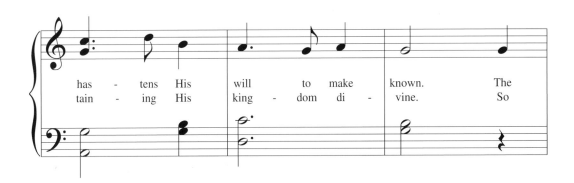

has - tens His will to make known. The
tain - ing His king - dom di - vine. So

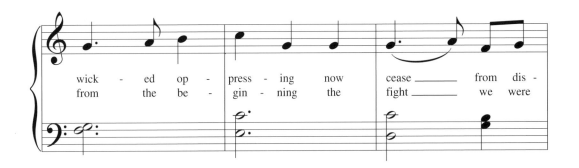

wick - ed op - press - ing now cease _____ from dis -
from the be - gin - ning the fight _____ we were

tress - ing. Sing prais - es to His name; _____ He for -
win - ning, thou, Lord, wast at our side; _____ all _____

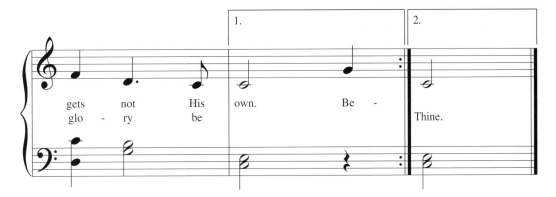

gets not His own. Be -
glo - ry be

2.
Thine.

Softly and Tenderly

Words and Music by
WILL L. THOMPSON

Moderately slow

Soft - ly and ten - der - ly Je - sus is call - ing,
Why should we tar - ry when Je - sus is plead - ing,

call - ing for you and for me.
plead - ing for you and for me?

Copyright © 2014 by HAL LEONARD CORPORATION
International Copyright Secured   All Rights Reserved

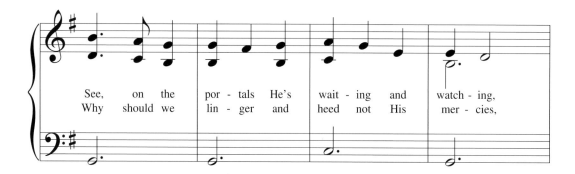

See, on the por - tals He's wait - ing and watch - ing,
Why should we lin - ger and heed not His mer - cies,

watch - ing for you and for me. ____ } Come
mer - cies for you and for me? ____

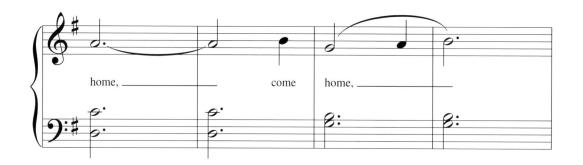

home, ____ come home, ____

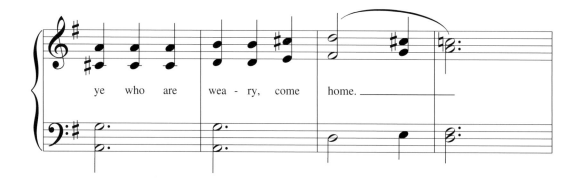

ye who are wea - ry, come home. ____

Ear - nest - ly, ten - der - ly, Je - sus is call - ing,

1.

call - ing, O sin - ner, come home!

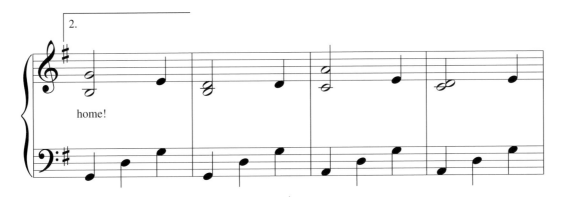

2.

home!

What a Friend We Have in Jesus

Words by JOSEPH M. SCRIVEN
Music by CHARLES C. CONVERSE

Slowly

What   a friend we have in
Have   we tri - als and temp-

Je - sus,   all   our sins and griefs to
ta - tions?   Is   there trou - ble an - y -

bear!   What   a pri - vi - lege to car - ry
where?   We should nev - er be dis - cour - aged,

Copyright © 1993 by HAL LEONARD CORPORATION
International Copyright Secured   All Rights Reserved

ev - 'ry-thing to God in prayer! Oh, what peace we of - ten
take it to the Lord in prayer! Can we find a friend so

for - feit, oh, what need-less pain we bear,
faith - ful, who will all our sor-rows share?

all be - cause we do not car - ry
Je - sus knows our ev - 'ry weak - ness,

ev - 'ry-thing to God in prayer.
take it to the Lord in

prayer. *rit.*

WHEN I SURVEY THE WONDROUS CROSS

Words by ISAAC WATTS
Music arranged by LOWELL MASON
Based on Plainsong

Moderately

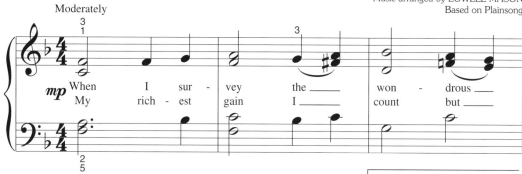

When I sur - vey the won - drous
My rich - est gain I count but

1.
cross on and which the Prince of
loss pour con -

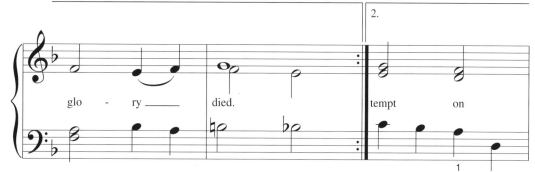

2.
glo - ry died. tempt on

all my pride.

Copyright © 2014 by HAL LEONARD CORPORATION
International Copyright Secured   All Rights Reserved